The Mueller Report Graphic Novel

by Barbara Slate

Volume 1
Report on the Investigation into Russian
Interference in the 2016 Presidential Election

Volume 2
Obstruction Inquiry

HUDSON, NEW YORK
RICHARD MINSKY
2019

Hardcover ISBN: 978-0-937258-11-8
Paperback ISBN: 978-0-937258-12-5

First Combined Edition

This graphic novel is based on the *Report on the Investigation into Russian Interference in the 2016 Presidential Election*, the official report documenting the findings and conclusions of Special Counsel Robert Mueller's investigation into Russian efforts to interfere in the 2016 United States presidential election, allegations of conspiracy or coordination between Donald Trump's presidential campaign and Russia, and allegations of obstruction of justice. A redacted version of the 448-page report was publicly released by the Department of Justice on April 18, 2019. It is divided into two volumes. This edition of *Mueller Report Graphic Novel* interprets and condenses the redacted report and is also issued in two volumes. This edition contains both volumes.

It began with a post...

Jennifer Taub ✔
April 18 🌐

Just had a copy made and bound for easier reading.

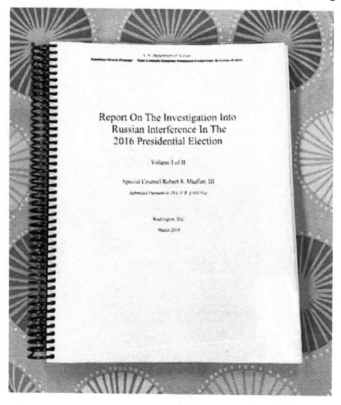

U. S. Department of Justice
Attorney Work Product // May Contain Material Protected Under Fed. R. Crim. P. 6(e)

Report On The Investigation Into
Russian Interference In The
2016 Presidential Election

Volume I of II

Special Counsel Robert S. Mueller, III

Submitted Pursuant to 28 C.F.R. § 600.8(c)

Washington, D.C.

March 2019

👍❤️😮 401

Barbara Slate Maybe I'll do a graphic novel about it!
Like   Reply

Jennifer Taub ✔ Barbara Slate
🤍 I can't wait til you create this

for Aunt Emily

CONTENTS

Volume 1

Volume 2

The Russian government interfered in the 2016 presidential election in sweeping and systematic fashion.

Robert S. Mueller, III

THE VOLUNTEER

The Internet Research Agency (IRA) carried out the earliest Russian interference operations— a social media campaign designed to provoke and amplify political and social discord in the United States. The IRA received funding from Russian oligarch Yevgeniy Prigozhin. Prigozhin is widely reported to have ties to Russian President Vladimir Putin.

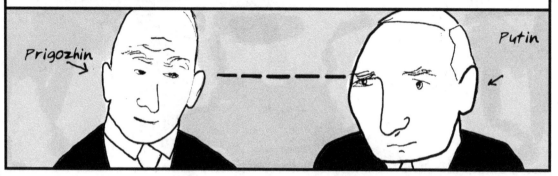

The IRA used social media accounts and interest groups to cause chaos through "information warfare." The campaign was to undermine the U.S. electoral system, a targeted operation that favored candidate Trump and disparaged candidate Clinton.

IRA staged political rallies inside the United States. To organize those rallies, IRA employees posed as U.S. grassroots entities and people, contacting Trump supporters and Campaign officials in the United States.

June 4, 2014, four IRA employees applied to the U.S. Department of State to enter the United States. They lied about their mission, claiming to be four friends who had met at a party. Anna Bogacheva and Aleksandra Krylova received visas and entered the United States. The IRA referred to these employees as "specialists."

Specialist Anna

Specialist Aleksandra

The GRU (Main Intelligence Directorate of the General Staff of the Russian Army) began hacking the email accounts of the Clinton Campaign. They stole hundreds of thousands of documents and disseminated the materials through fictitious online personas. The GRU later released additional materials through...

WIKILEAKS

[Organization that publishes news leaks, founded by Julian Assange]

IRA Facebook Groups popped up everywhere with names such as...

Being Patriotic
Stop all Immigrants
Secured Borders
Tea Party News
Black Matters
Blacktivist
Don't Shoot Us
LGBTQ United
United Muslims of America

A Facebook representative testified that Facebook had identified 140 IRA-controlled Facebook accounts that made 80,000 posts and reached 126 million people.

With one click, you could get a "Specialist" friend.

HOW TO ORGANIZE A RALLY IN 6 EASY STEPS

1. Get an IRA specialist to pose as a U.S. grassroots activist.

2. Use a social media persona to promote the rally.

3. Send direct messages to followers.

4. Get an enthused U.S. citizen follower to become an event coordinator.

5. Promote the rally by contacting U.S. media with the event coordinator.

6. Post videos and photographs and distribute to IRA vast social media.

Do it all over again.

Collectively, the IRA's social media accounts reached tens of millions of U.S. citizens. The IRA recruited unsuspecting citizens and criticized Clinton's record as Secretary of State. When the Clinton posts slowed down, a representative was there to remind the specialists.

It is imperative to intensify criticizing Hillary!

How about she's an alien?

Naw. We did that one already.

Candidate Trump's Facebook account posted about the August 20, 2016 political rallies organized by the IRA.

Donald J. Trump

Thank you for your support!. I love you - and

Seconds later...

LOOK! Mr. Trump posted about our event!

This is great!

The IRA also recruited individuals to perform political acts such as walking around New York City dressed up as Santa Claus with a Trump mask.

I redacted the image of Santa Trump. *You are welcome.*

THE HILLARY GAME

Whoever destroys her first wins. There are no rules.

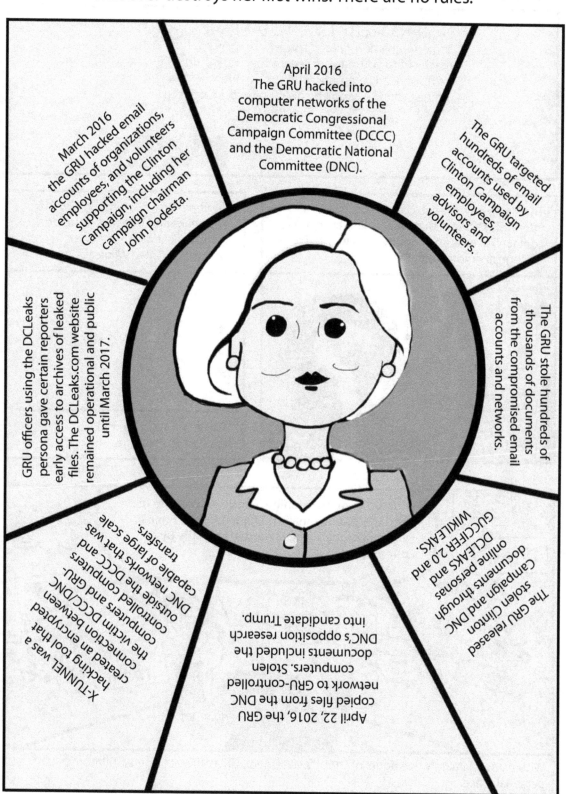

April 2016
The GRU hacked into computer networks of the Democratic Congressional Campaign Committee (DCCC) and the Democratic National Committee (DNC).

March 2016 the GRU hacked email accounts of organizations, employees, and volunteers supporting the Clinton Campaign, including her campaign chairman John Podesta.

The GRU targeted hundreds of email accounts used by Clinton Campaign employees, advisors and volunteers.

GRU officers using the DCLeaks persona gave certain reporters early access to archives of leaked files. The DCLeaks.com website remained operational and public until March 2017.

The GRU stole hundreds of thousands of documents from the compromised email accounts and networks.

X-TUNNEL was a hacking tool that created an encrypted connection between the victim DCCC/DNC controlled computers and GRU-controlled computers outside the DCCC and DNC networks that was capable of large scale transfers.

April 22, 2016, the GRU copied files from the DNC network to GRU-controlled computers. Stolen documents included the DNC's opposition research into candidate Trump.

The GRU released stolen Clinton Campaign and DNC documents through online personas DCLEAKS and GUCCIFER 2.0 and WIKILEAKS.

WIKILEAKS

Communications occurred between WikiLeaks and the GRU-operated persona DCLeaks. On September 15, 2016, @dcleaks wrote to @WikiLeaks...

> hi there! I'm from DC Leaks. How could we discuss some submission-related issues? Am trying to reach out to you via your secure chat but getting no response. I've got something that might interest you. You won't be disappointed, I promise.

> Hi there.

That same day, the Guccifer 2.0 persona informed DCLeaks that WikiLeaks was trying to contact DCLeaks and arrange for a way to speak through encrypted emails.

Beginning on September 20, 2016, WikiLeaks and DCLeaks resumed communications.
DCLeaks emailed Wikileaks...

> Hi from DCLeaks

The email contained a PGP*-encrypted message.

*Pretty Good Privacy

And soon...

> Russia, if you're listening, I hope you're able to find the 30,000 emails that are missing. I think you will probably be rewarded mightily by our press.

Within approximately five hours of Trump's statement, GRU officers targeted Clinton's personal office.

The Trump Campaign showed interest in WikiLeak's releases of hacked materials throughout the summer and fall of 2016. [Harm to Ongoing Matter]

In debriefings with the Office*, former deputy campaign chairman Rick Gates said that,

[Harm to Ongoing Matter]

[Harm to Ongoing Matter]

[Harm to Ongoing Matter] Gates recalled candidate Trump being generally frustrated that the Clinton emails had not been found.

Paul Manafort, who would later become campaign chairman, [Harm to Ongoing Matter]

[Harm to Ongoing Matter]

Michael Cohen, former executive vice president of the Trump Organization and special counsel to Donald J. Trump, told the Office that he recalled an incident in which he was in candidate Trump's office in Trump Tower [Harm to Ongoing Matter]

[Harm to Ongoing Matter]

[Harm to Ongoing Matter]

[Harm to Ongoing Matter] Cohen further told the Office that, after WikiLeak's subsequent release of stolen DNC emails in July 2016, candidate Trump said to Cohen something to the effect of, [Harm to Ongoing Matter]

According to Gates, by the late summer of 2016, the Trump Campaign was planning a press strategy, a communications campaign, and messaging based on the possible release of Clinton emails by WikiLeaks. [Harm to Ongoing Matter]

[Harm to Ongoing Matter]

[Harm to Ongoing Matter] while Trump and Gates were driving to LaGuardia Airport,

[Harm to Ongoing Matter] Shortly after the call candidate Trump told Gates that more releases of damaging information would be coming.

*Special Counsel's Office

On October 7, 2016, the Washington Post published an Access Hollywood video that captured comments by candidate Trump some years earlier. The tape was expected to adversely affect the campaign.

Less than an hour after the video's publication, WikiLeaks released the first set of emails stolen by the Russian Government from the account of Clinton Campaign Chairman John Podesta.

On October 3rd, 2016, Wikileaks sent a twitter direct message to Donald Trump, Jr.

A PAC run anti-Trump site is about to launch. It is focused on Trump's "unprecedented and dangerous" ties to Russia. We have guessed the password. It is 'putintrump.'

Trump Jr. emailed a variety of senior campaign staff.

Guys I got a weird Twitter DM from wikileaks. See below. I tried the password and it works. Not sure if this is anything but it seems like it's really wikileaks asking me as I follow them and it is a DM. Do you know the people mentioned and what the conspiracy they are looking for could be?

WikiLeaks sent another direct message to Trump Jr.

You guys, we need help to disseminate a link alleging candidate Clinton advocated using a drone to target Julian Assange, founder and director of WikiLeaks.

I already did.

October 12, 2016...

It was great to see you and your dad talking about our publications. Strongly suggest your dad tweets this link if he mentions us wlsearch.tk. It will help in "digging through" leaked emails. We just released Podesta emails Part 4.

Two days later, Trump Jr. tweeted out...

wlsearch.tk

15

Throughout 2016, the Trump Campaign expressed great interest in Hillary Clinton's private email server. Trump Campaign advisor Michael Caputo learned through a Florida-based Russian business partner that another Florida-based Russian, Henry Oknyansky (aka Henry Greenberg) claimed to have the goods.

BEGIN HERE:

Caputo notified Roger Stone, an American political consultant, and connected Stone and Oknyansky.

Oknyansky and Stone set up a May 2016 in-person meeting.

Oknyansky was accompanied to the meeting by Alexei Rasin, a Ukrainian associate involved in Florida real estate.

Smith wrote that there was a "tug-of-war going on within WikiLeaks over its planned releases in the next few days" and that WikiLeaks "will save its best revelations for last, under the theory this allows little time for response prior to the U.S. election November 8."

An attachment to the email claimed that WikiLeaks would release "All 33k deleted Emails" by "November 1st."

No emails obtained from Clinton's server were subsequently released.

Rasin offered to sell Stone derogatory info on Clinton. Stone refused.

Trump asked individuals affiliated with his campaign to find the deleted emails

The SEARCH FOR THE 30,000 MISSING EMAILS

Smith continued to send emails to an undisclosed recipient list about Clinton's deleted emails until shortly before the election.

Michael Flynn-who would later serve as National Security Advisor in the Trump Administration, recalled that he made this request repeatedly.

In early September 2016, Smith circulated a document stating that his initiative was "in coordination" with the Trump Campaign, "to the extent permitted as an independent expenditure organization." The document listed multiple individuals affiliated with the Trump campaign.

A backup of Smith's computer contained two files that had been downloaded from WikiLeaks and were originally attached to emails received by John Podesta.

Flynn contacted Senate staffer Barbara Ledeen (who began her efforts to obtain the emails in December 2015) and Peter Smith, an investment advisor.

September 2016, Smith and Ledeen got back in touch. Ledeen claimed to have obtained a trove of emails (from the "dark web") that purported to be the deleted Clinton emails. A tech advisor determined the emails were not authentic.

December 3, 2015, Ledeen emailed Smith a proposal to obtain the emails and attached a proposal stating "The Clinton email server was breached long ago. The Chinese, Russian and Iranian intelligence services could reassemble the server's email content.

Smith made claims that he was in contact with hackers with "ties and affiliations to Russia" who had access to the emails, and that his efforts were coordinated with the Trump campaign.

He created a company, raised tens of thousands of dollars, and recruited security experts and business associates.

Smith tried to locate and obtain the emails himself.

Smith forwarded the proposal to two colleagues. On December 16, 2015, Smith declined to participate in her "initiative."

TRUMPMOSCOW TOWER

September 2015, Felix Sater, a N.Y. real estate adviser, contacted Michael Cohen, executive vice president of the Trump Organization.

Buddy, let's do a TrumpMoscow Tower!

Cohen obtained approval from candidate Trump , who was then president of the Trump Organization. Cohen kept Trump up-to-date.

It's continuing, Boss.

Cohen consulted with Ivanka, Trump's daughter, about TrumpMoscow Tower...

I prefer Corinthian columns for my spa.

TrumpMoscow Project

...and Trump Jr., about his possible involvement.

I would be invaluable. I have so much Moscow experience.

On September 22, 2015, Cohen forwarded a preliminary design for TrumpMoscow to Giorgi Rtskhiladze, a Georgian-American executive who had pursued business ventures in Moscow.

Cohen wrote...

I look forward to your reply about this spectacular project in Moscow.

Rtskhiladze replied...

If we could organize the meeting in New York at the highest level of the Russian Government and Mr. Trump this project would definitely receive the worldwide attention.

Later, Rtskhiladze sent another email...

The TrumpMoscow Tower will be a symbol of stronger economic, business and cultural relationships between New York and Moscow and therefore United States and the Russian Federation.

Trump signed an LOI (Letter of Intent).

The LOI included...

residential, hotel, commercial, and office components,

250 first class luxury residential condominiums,

one first class luxury hotel consisting of approximately 15 floors and containing not fewer than 150 hotel rooms,

$4 million up front fee prior to ground breaking to the Trump Organization.

TRUMP
MOSCOW

On November 3, 2015, the day after the Trump Organization transmitted the LOI, Felix Sater emailed Cohen.

Buddy, our boy can become President of the USA and we can engineer it. I will get all of Putins team to buy in on this, I will manage this process. You and I will get Donald and Vladimir on a stage together very shortly.

Michael lets go. 2 boys from Brooklyn getting a USA president elected. This is good really good.

TAP TAP
TAP
TAP TAP

PAPADOPOULOS

In the summer of 2015, George Papadopoulos sought a role as a foreign policy advisor to the Trump campaign but was getting nowhere.

The Trump Campaign is not hiring policy advisors.

Papadopoulos persisted. At the time of a March 2 email, the Trump Campaign was getting criticized for lack of experienced foreign policy advisors.

The best...the smartest.

Who's your foreign team?

What's your policy?

What's your experience?

Later, Trump demanded...

GET ME A FOREIGN POLICY TEAM!

A campaign official gave Papadopoulos's name to Sam Clovis, Trump's chief policy advisor.

You have a role as a foreign policy advisor to the Trump Campaign. Russia will be important in the Campaign's foreign policy.

George Papadopoulos is the best and smartest.

Who?

How do you spell that?

Papadopoulos was a foreign policy advisor to the Campaign from March to October 2016.

In late April, Papadopoulos was told by London-based professor Joseph Mifsud that the Russian Government had "dirt" on Clinton in the form of thousands of emails. It could assist the Campaign through the anonymous release of information that would be damaging to candidate Clinton.

These connections could increase my importance as a policy advisor in the Trump administration.

Papadopoulos sent an email to members of the Trump Foreign policy advisory team. The subject line was "Meeting with Russian leadership—including Putin."

Just finished a very productive lunch with a good friend, Joseph Mifsud, the director of the London Academy of Diplomacy. The topic was to arrange a meeting between us and the Russian leadership. They are keen to host us in a "neutral" city or Moscow. Putin is ready to meet. Waiting for everyone's thoughts.

Clovis responded...

This is most informative. We probably should not go forward until we sit with our NATO allies. We need to reassure them that we are not going to advance anything with Russia until we have everyone on the same page.

More thoughts later today. Great work.

March 31, 2016 meeting of the foreign policy team, Papadopoulos spoke...

I have learned through my contacts in London that Putin wants to meet with Trump. My connections could help arrange a meeting.

Trump was interested and receptive to the idea of a meeting.

THE TRUMP TOWER MEETING

Donald Trump, Jr. got an email from Robert Goldstone, a British publicist and music manager, at the request of his client...

...Russian pop star Emin Agalarov, the son of...

...Aras Agalarov, a Russian billionaire businessman and property developer with ties to Putin.

Aras worked with Trump in connection with the 2013 Miss Universe pageant in Moscow. He arranged to get Putin a special invitation from Trump to attend the pageant.

Is he here yet?

But Putin was a no show.

Back in NYC, Aras's daughter delivered a special gift for Mr. Trump.

It's from Russia.

It was a black lacquered box. Inside was a sealed letter from Putin.

What the letter said has never been revealed.

The email to Donald Trump, Jr. from the music manager read...

Good morning,
Emin just called and asked me to contact you with something very interesting. The Crown prosecutor of Russia offered to provide the Trump Campaign with some official documents and information that would incriminate Hillary and her dealings with Russia and would be very useful to your father. This is very sensitive but is part of Russia and its government support for Trump.
Best,
Rob Goldstone

Minutes later Trump Jr. responded...

If it's what you say I love it

Trump Jr. and the pop star had multiple conversations. A meeting was in the works. Trump Jr. invited campaign chairman Paul Manafort and Senior advisor Jared Kushner to attend.

Much of the staff knew about the meeting. Cohen recalls Trump Jr. leaning in to tell Trump Senior the news...

According to written answers submitted by President Trump, he has no recollection of learning about the meeting.

June 9, 2016, Trump Tower...

Manafort   Trump Jr.   and Jared Kushner met with

Ike Kaveladze, VP of Aras Algarov's company

Natalia Veselnitskaya, a Russian attorney

Goldstone, the music manager

Samochornov, a translator

Akhmetshin, a Russian lobbyist

Natalia Veselnitskaya provided dirt.

Funds derived from illegal activities in Russia were provided to Hillary.

Trump Jr. wanted to know...

Do you have proof?

I lost track when the money arrived in the U. S.

but while we're on the subject, the Magnitsky Act* is unfair! Why impose sanctions on Russia when we have done nothing wrong?!

*Magnitsky Act: A 2012 U.S. statute that imposed financial and travel sanctions on Russian officials, which resulted in a retaliatory ban in Russia on U.S. adoptions of Russian children.

Kushner sent emails to assistants at Kushner Companies...

Call me. I need an excuse to get out of this meeting.

BRRRRING!!!

What?
Okay I'll be right there!

EMERGENCY!!!

The meeting quickly ended. It became public in July 2017.

There was a meeting at Trump Tower with at least 3 Russians. Donald Trump, Jr., Manafort, and Jared Kushner attended.

BREAKING NEWS

Don Jr. explained...

It was a nothing burger.

The next month Goldstone commented to Emin about the volume of publicity the June 9 meeting had generated...

Now the FBI is on it. My reputation is destroyed by this dumb meeting.

PUTIN HAS WON

Trump wanted to change his 2012 view...

RUSSIA IS THE NUMBER ONE THREAT TO OUR COUNTRY!

to his 2016 view...

LET'S BE FRIENDS.

During the week of the National Republican Convention (NRC) Trump campaign officials met with Russian Ambassador Sergey Kislyak, a Senior Russian diplomat and politician.

Soon after, J.D. Gordon, a senior advisor to the Trump Campaign, watered down a proposed amendment to the Republican party platform.

I request that "lethal" assistance to Ukraine in response to Russian aggression be changed to "appropriate" assistance.

U.S. arming Ukrainians in the fight against the pro-Russian forces was staunchly opposed by the Russian government.

Diana Denman, a Republican delegate who supported arming U.S. allies in Ukraine reported...

J.D. Gordon told me that Trump directed him to support weakening the position in the platform.

Ultimately, the watered down version was adopted. When Trump was asked about the reason for changing the amendment...

Amendment? What amendment?

March 2016 Donald Trump pronounced to Paul Manafort...

YOU'RE HIRED.

It is an honor, Sir. I'll work for free.

Mar-a-Lago

Paul Manafort served on the Trump Campaign, including as Campaign Chairman, from March to August 2016.

Manafort had connections to Russia through his prior work for Russian oligarch Oleg Vladimirovich Deripaska (OVD) a billionaire tycoon with close ties to Putin...

... and connections through work for a pro-Russian regime in Ukraine.

OVD filed a suit in New York State court claiming Manafort and Rick Gates, Manafort's deputy on the Campaign and longtime assistant, defrauded him of $18.9 million.

NEW YORK STATE COURT

Manafort was concerned.

How am I ever going to pay OVD back?

Manafort told Gates to provide Kilimnik, a Russian/Ukrainian political consultant and Russian intelligence operative, with updates on the Trump Campaign.

Kilimnik

Manafort expected Kilimnik to share the information with OVD, and with three Ukrainian oligarchs.

Akhmetov

Serhiy Lyovochkin

Boris Kolesnikov

Manafort emailed Kilimnik.

Have you shown "our friends" the media coverage of my new role?

Absolutely. Every article.

How do we use to get whole. Has **OVD** operation seen?

Yes I have been sending everything

April 2016 Manafort instructed Gates to send internal polling data prepared for the Trump campaign.

Gates then deleted communications on a daily basis.

DELETE

Manafort emailed Kilimnik.

Any movement on this issue with our friend?

I am carefully optimistic on the question of our biggest interest.

If he needs private briefings we can accommodate.

Manafort met with Kilimnik to discuss 3 issues. First, a plan to resolve the political problems in Ukraine. This included a "backdoor" means for Russia to control eastern Ukraine. Kilimnik told Manafort...

All we need is a wink and perhaps a nudge from DT.

Second, Manafort briefed Kilimnik on the state of the Trump campaign.

BATTLEGROUND STATES

Michigan
Wisconsin
Pennsylvania
Minnesota

Third, they discussed two financial matters: the lawsuit, and 2 mil owed to Manafort for consulting work for Ukrainians. Manafort was concerned.

Come on. I've given them millions worth of info. You gotta get OVD to drop this damn lawsuit.

The press started tracking Manafort.

NEWS

MANAFORT SHARED 2016 DATA WITH RUSSIAN PAL

Manafort had to resign from the Trump Campaign.

It's been a pleasure to serve.

TRUMP

Trump acknowledged Manafort's fine work.

I am very appreciative for his great work in helping to get us where we are today, and in particular his work guiding us through the delegate and convention process. Paul is a true professional and I wish him the greatest success.

Although no longer part of the team, Manafort continued to offer advice to campaign officials.

At approximately 2:40 a.m. on November 9, 2016 news reports stated that

Investigative Technique

wrote to Dmitriev, "Putin has won."

3 a.m. on election night, Hope Hicks, Trump's press secretary, received a call.

Brrring!

The person sounded foreign. Although Hope had a hard time understanding, she could make out the words.

Putin call.

The next day, Sergey Kuznetsov, an official at the Russian Embassy, emailed Hope with an attachment... SUBJECT: Message from Putin.

Congratulations.

I look forward to working with you on heading Russian American relations out of crisis.

Hope forwarded the email to Kushner.

Can you look into this? Don't want to get duped but don't want to blow off Putin!

And soon...

Hope, it's Putin.

Five days later, Trump and Putin spoke by phone.

Vladimir!

Trump.

On November 30, 2016, Kushner met at Trump Tower with Kislyak, the Russian Ambassador, and Michael Flynn, National Security Advisor. Kushner began...

We would like to start afresh with U.S. Russian relations...

TRUMP

I will need someone to communicate with who has direct contact with Putin and the ability to speak for him.

Kislyak arranged for Kushner to meet with Sergey Gorkov, head of the Russian-government-owned bank Vnesheconombank (VEB) with a very close connection to Vladimir Putin.

When The Office asked what was discussed at that high level meeting with Gorkov, Kushner responded...

Meeting? With Gorkov? We never even bothered to google his name.

Two months before the election U.S. intelligence officials concluded that Putin was directly involved in his government's efforts to meddle in the election. Sept. 5, 2016, President Barack Obama warned Putin...

Cut it out.

The warning went unheeded. After the election, President Obama signed an Executive Order imposing many sanctions on Russia:

Imposed sanctions on nine Russian individuals and entities.

Expelled thirty-five Russian government officials.

Closed two Russian government-owned compounds in the U.S.

In a meeting at Mar-a-Lago, senior officials and President Elect Trump were concerned that these sanctions would harm U.S. relations with Russia.

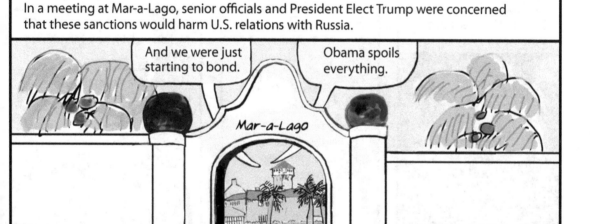

And we were just starting to bond.

Obama spoils everything.

Mar-a-Lago

The Press wanted to know...

Are you imposing sanctions on Russia?

I think we ought to get on with our lives.

Incoming National Security Advisor Michael Flynn was the primary conduit for communications with Russian Ambassador Kislyak.

Flynn was anxiously waiting to hear from the Mar-a-Lago team as to how to handle the sanctions. Flynn got word.

Make sure the situation does not get out of hand.

Flynn called Kislyak.

Don't do a tit for tat.

Soon Putin released a statement.

Russia will not take retaliatory measures in response to the sanctions at this time.

Trump tweeted...

Donald J. Trump ✔
@realDonaldTrump

Great move on delay (by V. Putin). I always knew he was smart.

At a briefing, Trump asked K.T. McFarland, Flynn's incoming deputy...

Was it the Russians?   Yes.

It could be the Russians or it could also be somebody sitting on their bed that weighs 400 pounds.

WE ♥ TRUMP

MINERS FOR TRUMP

WOMEN 4 TRUMP

On July 13, 2018, a federal grand jury returned an indictment charging Russian military intelligence officers with conspiring to hack into U.S. computers used by the Clinton Campaign, DNC, DCCC, steal documents from those computers, and stage releases of the stolen documents to interfere in the election. The indictment also describes how, in staging the releases, the defendants used the Guccifer 2.0 persona to disseminate documents through WikiLeaks; and a separate conspiracy to hack into the computers of U.S. persons and entities responsible for the administration of the 2016 U.S. election.

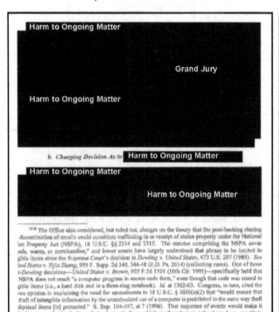

Harm to Ongoing Matter

Grand Jury

Harm to Ongoing Matter

b. Charging Decision As to Harm to Ongoing Matter

Harm to Ongoing Matter

Harm to Ongoing Matter

[1209] The Office also considered, but ruled out, charges on the theory that the post-hacking sharing dissemination of emails could constitute trafficking in or receipt of stolen property under the National len Property Act (NSPA), 18 U.S.C. §§ 2314 and 2315. The statutes comprising the NSPA cover ods, wares, or merchandise," and lower courts have largely understood that phrase to be limited to gible items since the Supreme Court's decision in *Dowling v. United States*, 473 U.S. 207 (1985). *See* ted *States v. Yijia Zhang*, 995 F. Supp. 2d 340, 344-48 (E.D. Pa. 2014) (collecting cases). One of those t-*Dowling* decisions—*United States v. Brown*, 925 F.2d 1301 (10th Cir. 1991)—specifically held that NSPA does not reach "a computer program in source code form," even though that code was stored in gible items (i.e., a hard disk and in a three-ring notebook). *Id.* at 1302-03. Congress, in turn, cited the ven opinion in explaining the need for amendments to 18 U.S.C. § 1030(a)(2) that "would ensure that theft of intangible information by the unauthorized use of a computer is prohibited in the same way theft physical items [is] protected." S. Rep. 104-357, at 7 (1996). That sequence of events would make it ïcult to argue that hacked emails in electronic form, which are the relevant stolen items here, constitute ods, wares, or merchandise" within the meaning of the NSPA.

176

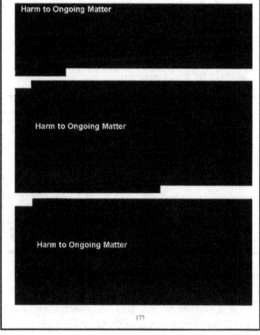

Harm to Ongoing Matter

Harm to Ongoing Matter

Harm to Ongoing Matter

177

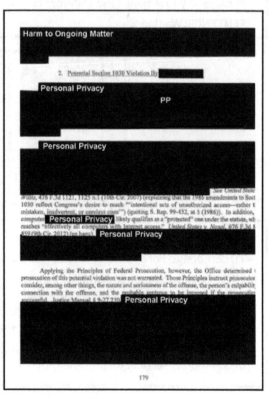

Harm to Ongoing Matter

2. Potential Section 1030 Violation By [Personal Privacy]

Personal Privacy

PP

Personal Privacy

See United State
[*v.] IHG*, 476 F.3d 1121, 1125 n.1 (10th Cir. 2007) (explaining that the 1986 amendments to Sect 1030 reflect Congress's desire to reach "'intentional acts of unauthorized access—rather t mistaken, inadvertent, or careless ones'") (quoting S. Rep. 99-432, at 5 (1986)). In addition, computer Personal Privacy likely qualifies as a "protected" one under the statute, wh reaches "effectively all computers with Internet access." *United States v. Nosal*, 676 F.3d 1 859 (9th Cir. 2012) (en banc). Personal Privacy

Applying the Principles of Federal Prosecution, however, the Office determined prosecution of this potential violation was not warranted. Those Principles instruct prosecutor consider, among other things, the nature and seriousness of the offense, the person's culpabilit connection with the offense, and the probable sentence to be imposed if the prosecutio successful. Justice Manual § 9-27.230. Personal Privacy

179

Harm to Ongoing Matter

Harm to Ongoing Matter

Harm to Ongoing Matter

Harm to Ongoing Matter

[Ha]rm to Ongoing Matter

178

Although the evidence of contacts between Trump Campaign officials and Russia-affiliated individuals may not have been sufficient to establish or sustain criminal charges, several U.S. persons connected to the campaign made false statements about those contacts and took other steps to obstruct the Office's investigation and those of Congress. The office therefore charged some of those individuals with making false statements and obstructing justice.

NAME: Paul Manafort

TITLE: Campaign Chairman for Trump Campaign

CONSPIRACY: (1) to defraud the United States and to commit offenses against the United States, and (2) to obstruct justice (witness tampering).

SENTENCE: 73 months

NAME: Rick Gates

TITLE: Manafort deputy

CONSPIRACY: to defraud and commit multiple offenses against the United States, and making false statements to the Office.

PLEA: Guilty—struck a deal

NAME: Michael Flynn

TITLE: National Security Advisor to the President

LIE: Content of conversations with Kislyak when U.S. had imposed sanctions on Russia.

PLEA: Guilty to making false statements

SENTENCE: Waiting

NAME: Michael Cohen

TITLE: Executive Vice-president and special counsel to the Trump Organization

LIE: when the Trump Moscow project ended, to minimize the links between the project and Trump (who by this time was president).

SENTENCE: 3 years

NAME: George Papadopoulos

TITLE: Foreign Policy advisor to the Trump Campaign

LIES: Timing, extent and nature of communications with the Russians, lying that communications occurred before joining the Trump Campaign.

PLEA: Guilty to making false statements to the FBI.

SENTENCE: 14 days in prison, $9,500 fine , 200 hours of community service.

Volume 2

Obstruction Inquiry

The obstruction-of-justice statute:

Whoever corruptly — (1) alters, destroys, mutilates, or conceals a record, document, or other object, or attempts to do so, with the intent to impair the object's integrity or availability for use in an official proceeding; or (2) otherwise obstructs, influences, or impedes any official proceeding, or attempts to do so, shall be fined under this title or imprisoned not more than 20 years, or both.

TRUMPMOSCOW CONNECTION

On June 16th, 2015, Donald Trump and his wife Melania rode down the escalator of Trump Tower...

...for a special announcement.

I am seeking the nomination as the Republican candidate for President.

By 2016, Trump distinguished himself from other Republican candidates by speaking of closer ties with Russia.

Putin and I could be friends. He is a strong leader.

The media reported on Trump campaign advisors with ties to Russia.

Campaign advisor Michael Flynn was seated next to Vladimir Putin at a gala in Moscow and also appeared regularly on Russian TV.

Foreign policy advisor Carter Page had ties to a Russian state-run gas company.

Campaign Chairman Paul Manafort had done work for the Russian-backed former Ukrainian president.

BREAKING NEWS

A cybersecurity firm for the DNC* announced Russian government hackers infiltrated the DNC's computer and obtained access to documents.

Only Russia's senior-most officials could have authorized these activities based on their scope and sensitivity.

*Democratic National Committee

John Podesta, Clinton's campaign manager, announced...

Russia hacked the DNC emails and arranged their release in order to help Trump.

The Times reported...

The New York Times
July 26, 2016
U.S. INTELLIGENCE CONFIDENT RUSSIANS BEHIND THEFT OF EMAILS TO SUPPORT TRUMP

Trump tweeted...

> **Donald J. Trump** ✓
> @realDonaldTrump
>
> **Crazy to suggest that Russia is dealing with Trump. For the record, I have ZERO investments in Russia.**

Here's an update on the TRUMPMOSCOW project, Boss.

TrumpMoscow
Ivanka Spa

Do you think you might say something about this project, Boss?

Why mention it if it's not a deal?

The Trump Campaign reacted to the Russian interference by distancing itself from Russia.

Foreign policy advisor J.D. Gordon declined an invite to Russian Ambassador Sergey Kislyak's residence.

Sorry Serge. Bad timing.

Manafort was asked to resign amid media coverage scrutinizing his ties to Russia.

When the media covered Carter Page's connections, Trump Campaign officials were in a quandary.

Never heard of him.

Did he get the coffee?

Trump announced...

This whole thing with Russia is a total deflection... far-fetched... ridiculous.

The opinion that Russia had hacked emails is unproven. It could be a 400 pound guy lying on a bed somewhere.

Will you be recognizing Crimea as Russian territory and consider lifting sanctions?

We'll be looking into that. Yeah, we'll be looking.

What are your ties to Russia?

I have nothing to do with Russia.

On October 7, 2016, WikiLeaks released the first set of emails stolen by a Russian intelligence agency from Clinton Campaign chairman John Podesta. Podesta said...

The FBI is investigating Russia's hacking. Trump might have known that the hacked emails were going to be released.

Vice Presidential Candidate Pence was asked...

Is the Trump Campaign in cahoots with WikiLeaks?

Nothing could be further from the truth.

On November 8, 2016, Trump was elected President. January 20, 2017 he was sworn in.

Hope Hicks, Trump Campaign spokesperson, spoke.

Chief of Staff Reince Priebus appeared on Fox News.

Was there any contact or coordination between the Trump Campaign and the Russians?

Even this question is insane. Of course we didn't interface with the Russians.

This whole thing is a spin job. The real question is, why the Democrats are doing everything they can to delegitimize the outcome of the election.

FOX NEWS

The President weighed in.

The Dems with this Russian interference thing is because they suffered one of the greatest defeats in the history of politics.

Reporters reported.

U.S. intelligence agencies have concluded Russia interfered in the presidential election to boost Donald Trump's bid for the White House.

BREAKING NEWS

The President was worried. He shared his concern with his trusted staff.

Will the people question the legitimacy of my historic win?

THE MESS FLYNN IS IN

On January 26, 2017, Acting Attorney General Sally Yates contacted White House Counsel Donald McGahn to discuss a sensitive matter.

Public statements made by the Vice President denying that Flynn and Kislyak discussed sanctions were not true.

That puts Flynn in a potentially compromised position because the Russians would know he lied.

By the way, Flynn has been interviewed by the FBI.

After the meeting McGahn called John Eisenberg, legal adviser to the National Security Council, and told him what Yates had said.

Can you get back to me on the mess Flynn is in?

That afternoon McGahn notified the President.

Sally Yates came to see me about Flynn. She said public statements made by the Vice President denying that Flynn and Kislyak discussed sanctions were not true and that Flynn has been interviewed by the FBI.

Can you repeat that?

McGahn repeated it.

Work with Priebus and Bannon and don't discuss it with anyone.

Flynn, not again.

this guy...

this stuff.

Meanwhile, Eisenberg informed McGahn...

There's a possibility that Flynn violated the Logan Act.*

* The Logan Act: A United States federal law that criminalizes negotiation by unauthorized persons with foreign governments having a dispute with the United States.

McGahn met again with Yates.

I doubt the Department of Justice would bring a Logan Act prosecution against Flynn, and we don't want to interfere with an ongoing FBI investigation.

That's why the Department of Justice notified the White House, so that it would take action.

McGahn ended the meeting.

Just one more thing. Could you get me the material the Department of Justice possesses on Flynn's discussions with Kislyak?

DINNER FOR 2

*Federal Bureau of Investigation

Later that night...

Meanwhile, McGahn and Priebus reviewed the material they received from the DOJ. Priebus told Flynn...

You have to resign.

I want to say good-bye to the President.

We'll give you a good recommendation. You're a good guy. We'll take care of you.

PAT PAT

On February 14, 2017, the day after Flynn's resignation, the President had lunch with New Jersey Governor Chris Christie.

Now that we fired Flynn, the Russia thing is over.

Hahahaha No way. This Russia thing is far from over.

What do you mean? Flynn met with the Russians. That was the problem. I fired Flynn. It's over.

You will never be able to get rid of Flynn. Like gum on the bottom of your shoe.

Later that day the President met with Comey, Sessions, and other officials for a briefing.

At the end of the briefing the President dismissed everyone except Comey.

Oh No! Not again.

I want to talk about Flynn. He did nothing wrong but he had to go because he lied to the Vice President.

Flynn is a good guy. He's been through a lot. I hope you can see your way clear to letting this go. He is a good guy. I hope you can let this go.

Shortly after the meeting Comey drafted a memorandum documenting the conversation.

I hope you can see your way clear to letting this go. He is a good guy. I hope you can let this go.

Comey also met with Andrew McCabe and other senior leaders to discuss the President's request.

Don't tell the staff that is investigating Flynn. We don't want them to be influenced as they continue their work.

And finally Comey went to see Sessions.

Please don't leave me alone with the President again.

SESSIONS WITH SESSIONS

In his January confirmation hearing to become Attorney General, Senator Sessions had not disclosed two meetings he had with Russian Ambassador Kislyak before the election, leading to congressional calls for Sessions to recuse.

BREAKING NEWS

The President called McGahn...

Get Sessions. Tell him not to recuse from the Russia investigation.

McGahn understood the President's concern.

A recusal would make Sessions look guilty for omitting details...

leaving the President unprotected from an investigation that could hobble the presidency...

and detract from the favorable press coverage for his Presidential Address to Congress.

McGahn reached out to Sessions.

The President is not happy about the possibility of a recusal.

I plan to follow the rules.

McGahn reported to the President about the conversation he had with Sessions. The President reiterated...

I DO NOT WANT HIM TO RECUSE.

Throughout the day, McGahn continued trying to avert Sessions's recusal. He spoke to Sessions's personal counsel, Sessions's chief of staff, Jody Hunt and Senate Majority Leader, Mitch McConnell.

He's recusing.

PRIVAT

He's recusing.

Jeff's recusing.

That afternoon, Sessions announced...

I recuse from any existing or future investigations of any matters related in any way to the campaigns for President of the United States.

The day after Sessions's recusal, McGahn was called into the Oval Office.

I don't have a lawyer. I wish Roy Cohn was my lawyer. He knew how to get things done.

I need protection! Sessions is weak! Robert Kennedy and Eric Holder protected their presidents! You're telling me Bobby and Jack didn't talk about investigations? Or Obama tell Eric Holder who to investigate?!

That weekend, Sessions and McGahn flew to Mar-a-Lago to meet with the President. The President pulled Sessions aside to speak to him alone.

You want me to unrecuse my recusal?

LIFT THE CLOUD

On March 20, 2017 James Comey Jr., head of the F.B.I., announced...

The F.B.I. is investigating Russian interference in the 2016 election.

The President raged to his staff.

If people think Russia helped with the election it will take away from my historic victory.

The President reached out to the Director of National Intelligence (DNI) and leaders of the Central Intelligence Agency (CIA) and the National Security Agency (NSA) to ask them what they could do publicly to dispel the suggestion that the President had any connection to the Russian election-interference effort. But they all answered...

I cannot comment on the investigation.

I cannot comment on the investigation.

I cannot comment on the investigation.

Although White House advisors advised...

Any direct contact with the F.B.I. could be perceived as improper interference in an ongoing investigation.

...the President reached out to Comey.

Jim, it's the President. Announce that the President is not under investigation. Lift the cloud of the Russia investigation.

But Comey did not lift the cloud.

Is the President under investigation?

I cannot answer that.

And at the May 3, 2017 Senate Judiciary hearing Comey did not do any cloud lifting.

Is the President under investigation?

I'm not saying another word until the investigation is complete.

Following Comey's testimony the President met with McGahn, Sessions and Sessions's chief of staff Jody Hunt.

This is terrible, Jeff. It's all because you recused.

AG* is supposed to be the most important appointment. Kennedy appointed his brother. Obama appointed Holder. I appointed you and you recused!

*AG: Attorney General

I had no choice. It was a mandatory rather than discretionary decision.

You left me on an island. I can't do anything.

Sessions suggested...

A new start at the FBI would be appropriate. You should consider replacing Comey as FBI director.

Later that day, Trump bounced the idea to his trusted friend Steve Bannon.

You can't fire Comey, Donald. That ship has sailed.

Comey told me 3 times that I'm not under investigation. He's a showboater. He's a grandstander. I don't know any Russians. There was no collusion.

Firing Comey is not going to stop the investigation. You can fire the F.B.I. director but you can't fire the F.B.I.

TERMINATING COMEY

The weekend following Comey's testimony, the President traveled to his resort in Bedminster, New Jersey with family members and advisors. At dinner he shared...

The President dictated arguments and specific language for the Comey termination letter while Steve Miller, the President's political advisor, took notes.

Miller worked into the night, preparing the termination letter. He knew what to write.

Back at the Oval Office, the President met with senior advisors McGahn, Priebus, and Miller.

I am terminating Comey. The decision has been made.

The President read aloud from the termination letter.

Dear Director Comey, While I greatly appreciate your informing me, on three separate occasions, that I am not under investigation concerning the fabricated and politically-motivated allegations of a Trump-Russia relationship with respect to the 2016 Presidential Election, please be informed that I, along with members of both political parties and, most importantly, the American Public, have lost faith in you as the Director of the FBI and you are hereby terminated.

Comey Termination Draft

Mr. President, I'm having some trouble with the wording.

In an effort to slow down the decision, McGahn offered...

I heard the DOJ leadership is discussing Comey's status. We should talk to Rod* and Sessions and see what they have to say.

McGahn and White House Counsel Uttam Dhillon met with Sessions and Rosenstein.

I don't like the way he handled the Hillary emails.

I have no objection.

*Rod Rosenstein: the newly confirmed Deputy Attorney General.

The President and White House officials met with Sessions and Rosenstein. The President distributed copies of the updated termination letter and began the meeting.

I watched Comey's testimony over the weekend and thought that something was not right with him. He needs to go.

McGahn and Dhillon urged...

Let Comey resign.

No. I'm going to fire him.

The Officials discussed the mechanics of how to and what to say about the firing.

Let's go with his Hillary email decision.

That's an oldie but goodie!

I'm not sure we should use the President's letter at all.

What if Rob and Sessions recommend in writing that Comey should be removed?

Sean Spicer, the press secretary, released a statement.

THE WHITE HOUSE
Office of the Press Secretary

FOR IMMEDIATE RELEASE
May 9, 2017

Statement from the Press Secretary

Today, President Donald J. Trump informed FBI Director James Comey that he has been terminated and removed from office. President Trump acted based on the clear recommendations of both Deputy Attorney General Rod Rosenstein and Attorney General Jeff Sessions.

"The FBI is one of our Nation's most cherished and respected institutions and today will mark a new beginning for our crown jewel of law enforcement," said President Trump.

That evening, F.B.I. Deputy director Andrew McCabe was summoned to meet with the President at the White House.

I fired Comey because of the way he handled the Hillary emails and many other reasons. Were you aware that Comey told me 3 times that I was not under investigation?

Yes.

Do many people in the F.B.I. dislike Comey? Are you part of the resistance?

Most people in the F.B.I. feel positively about Comey. I worked closely with him.

Later that night, the President reached out to his old pal Chris Christie.

I'm getting killed in the press over Comey's termination!

Did you fire Comey because of what Rod wrote in the memo?

Yes.

Get Rod out there. Have him defend the decision.

The White House Press Office called the DOJ and said they wanted to put out a statement that it was Rosenstein's idea to fire Comey. Rosenstein replied...

I will not put out a false story.

DEPARTMENT OF JUSTICE

The President called Rod...

How about a press conference?

I don't think that's a good idea, Sir. If they ask, I would answer truthfully that it wasn't my idea.

Late in the evening, Spicer told reporters...

It was all Rosenstein. No one from the White House. It was a DOJ decision.

Deputy press secretary Sarah Sanders addressed the press.

The President, the Department of Justice, and bipartisan members of Congress had lost confidence in Comey. And most importantly, the rank and file of the FBI had lost confidence in Comey.

The President accepted the recommendation of his Deputy Attorney General to remove James Comey. Rosenstein decided *on his own* to review Comey's performance and decided *on his own* to come to the President.

A vast majority of the F.B.I. agents supported Comey.

Look, we've heard from countless members of the F.B.I. that say very different things.

When interviewed by the Special Counsel's Office, Sanders said that her reference to countless members of the FBI was a "slip of the tongue," and that the rank and file FBI agents had lost confidence in Comey was a comment she made "in the heat of the moment" that was not founded on anything.

Rosenstein and Sessions went to see McGahn.

I object.

It wasn't Rod's decision.

McGahn agreed and asked attorneys in the White House Counsel's Office to work with the press office to correct the narrative.

NOW who's to blame?

The next day the President participated in an interview with Lester Holt.

I made the decision to fire Comey before I met with Rosenstein and Sessions. I was going to fire regardless of recommendation. I was going to fire Comey knowing there was no good time to do it. And in fact, when I decided to just do it, I said to myself— I said, you know, this Russia thing with Trump and Russia is a made-up story. It's an excuse by the Democrats for having lost an election that they should've won.

NBC NEWS

The day before the Lester Holt interview, President Trump met with Russian Foreign Minister Sergey Lavrov and Russian Ambassador Sergey Kislyak in the Oval Office.

I just fired the head of the FBI. He was crazy, a real nut job. I faced great pressure because of Russia.

That's taken off. I'm not under investigation.

On May 17, 2017, Acting Attorney General Rosenstein appointed Robert S. Mueller, III as Special Counsel.

Robert S. Mueller, III is hereby authorized to conduct an Investigation into Russian interference in the 2016 presidential election.

The President, Sessions, Hunt, and McGahn were in the Oval Office looking at candidates to replace Comey when...

Bzzz Buzzz...

Excuse me, Mr. President. I have to take this call.

Jeff, it's me, Rod. I appointed a Special Counsel.

uh oh

Mr. President. Rosenstein appointed a Special Counsel to look into Russian interference in the election.

Oh my God. This is terrible.

This is the end of my Presidency.

I'm fucked.

May 18, Sessions finalized a resignation letter. Sessions, accompanied by Hunt, brought the letter to the White House and handed it to the President.

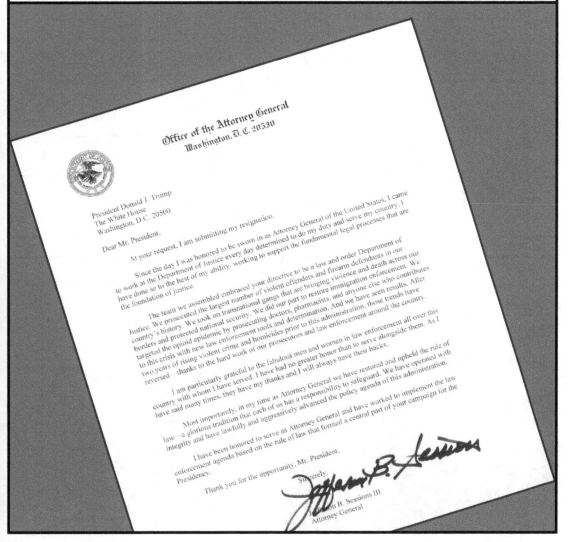

The President took the resignation letter and put it in his pocket.

Do you want to stay?

Yes Sir.

Do you want to continue serving as Attorney General?

Yes Sir, but that is up to you.

I want you to stay.

When Priebus and Bannon learned that the President was holding onto Session's resignation letter, they were concerned.

That could be used to influence the department of justice.

We gotta get that letter back.

Priebus contacted Sessions.

It's not good for the President to have the letter. It functions as a kind of shock collar. The President has the DOJ by the throat.

On May 19, 2017, the President left for a trip to the Middle East.

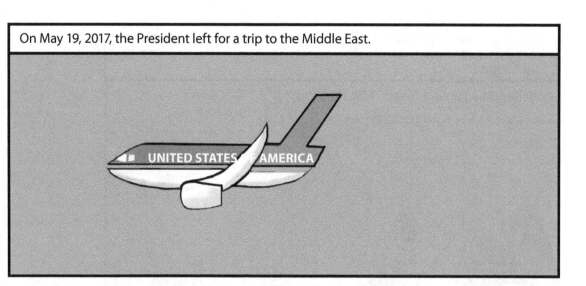

He shared with his senior advisors.

I got Sessions's resignation letter.

During the trip Priebus asked...

Since Sessions is not resigning, it would be a good idea to give me the resignation letter so I can return it to Jeff.

The letter is back at the White house.

Back at the White House, Priebus tried again.

It would be a really good idea to give me the resignation letter.

It's back at the hotel.

May 30, three days after the President returned from the trip, he returned the letter to Sessions with a notation saying...

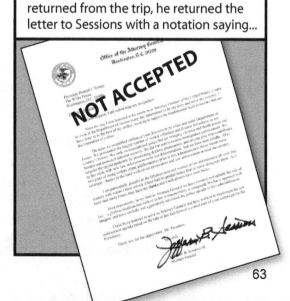

In the days following the Special Counsel's appointment, the President repeatedly told advisors that Mueller had conflicts of interest. The President told Priebus…

Mueller interviewed for the FBI director!

That doesn't count as a conflict.

He complained to McGahn…

He worked for a law firm that represented people affiliated with the President!

Nope. No conflict.

And bemoaned to Bannon…

Mueller disputed fees for his membership at my Trump golf course in Virginia!

That's ridiculous and petty.

The President persisted and told McGahn...

Reach out to Rosenstein. Tell him about the Mueller conflicts!

I will not call Rosenstein and I strongly advise you don't either.

It would look like trying to meddle in the investigation, and knocking out Mueller would be another fact used to claim obstruction of justice.

On June 8, 2017, Comey testified before Congress about his interactions with the President.

He wanted me to lift the cloud over his presidency caused by the investigation.

The President asked for my loyalty.

The President wanted me to let Flynn go.

The media reported Comey's recollections. Trump responded...

Loyalty? I hardly know the man. Why would I ask for his loyalty?

James Comey better hope there are no tapes of our conversations before he starts leaking to the press.

Comey answered...

Lordy! I hope there are.

YOU GOTTA CALL ROD

June 14, 2017, the Washington Post published an article stating that the Special Counsel was investigating whether the President had attempted to obstruct justice. This was the first public report that the President himself was under investigation by the Special Counsel's Office. Beginning early the next day, the President issued a series of tweets...

Donald J. Trump ✅
@realDonaldTrump

They made up a phony collusion with the Russians story, found zero proof, so now they go for obstruction of justice on the phony story. Nice.

Donald J. Trump ✅
@realDonaldTrump

You are witnessing the single greatest WITCH HUNT in American political history — led by some very bad and conflicted people!

Donald J. Trump ✅
@realDonaldTrump

After 7 months of investigations & committee hearings about my collusion with the Russians, nobody has been able to show any proof. Sad!

Donald J. Trump ✅
@realDonaldTrump

Crooked H destroyed phones w/ hammer, 'bleached' emails, & had husband meet w/AG days before she was cleared — & they talk about obstruction?

Donald J. Trump ✅
@realDonaldTrump

and I am being investigated for firing the FBI Director by the man who told me to fire the FBI Director! Witch Hunt.

On Saturday, June 17, 2017, the President called McGahn twice from Camp David. The first time...

Call Rosenstein and say that Mueller has conflicts of interest. He cannot serve as Special Counsel.

and then the second...

Have the special counsel removed!

Call Rod, Tell him Mueller has to go. Call me back when you do it.

I can't call Rod. That would be obstruction.

But what do I tell the President when he calls?

There's only one thing I can do.

McGahn called his personal lawyer, and then called his chief of staff Annie Donaldson.

I'm resigning. The President wants me to do something I don't want to do.

He drove to the office to pack his belongings and submit a resignation letter.

Later, McGahn called Priebus and Bannon and told them that he intended to resign.

The President asked me to do crazy shit.

Around the same time, the President called his old pal Chris Christie who advised...

There is no substantive basis to fire the Special Counsel. You would lose support from Republicans in Congress if you do.

Priebus and Bannon both urged McGahn not to quit, and McGahn ultimately returned to work that Monday and remained in his position. The President did not ask McGahn whether he had followed through with calling Rosenstein and didn't know that McGahn had planned to resign.

MESSAGE TO SESSIONS

On June 19, 2017, the President met in the Oval Office with his trusted former campaign manager Corey R. Lewandowski.

I want you to deliver a message to Sessions.

Tell him to give a public speech. Write this down.

I know that I recused myself from certain things having to do with specific areas. But our POTUS is being treated very unfairly. He shouldn't have a Special Prosecutor because he hasn't done anything wrong. I was on the campaign with him for nine months, there were no Russians involved with him. I know it for a fact because I was there. He didn't do anything wrong except he ran the greatest campaign in American history.

And tell Sessions he should meet with the Special Counsel to limit his jurisdiction to future elections.

If Sessions delivers that statement he would be the most popular guy in the country.

I understand, Sir. I'll get the message to Sessions.

Lewandowski wanted to pass the message to Sessions in person rather than over the phone. Lewandowski called Sessions and arranged a meeting for the following evening at Lewandowski's office, but Sessions had to cancel due to a last minute conflict.

Lewandowski did not want to meet at the Department of Justice because he did not want a public log of his visit and did not want Sessions to have an advantage over him by meeting on Sessions's turf.

Lewandowski left Washington, D.C., without having had an opportunity to meet with Sessions to convey the President's message.

Lewandowski stored the sensitive notes in a safe at his home.

Lewandowski contacted Rick Dearborn, then a senior White House official, and asked if he'd take a message to Sessions. Lewandowski believed Dearborn would be a better messenger because he had a longstanding relationship with Sessions and because Dearborn was in the government while Lewandowski was not.

Dearborn agreed without knowing what the message was, and Lewandowski later confirmed that Dearborn would meet with Sessions for dinner in late July and could deliver the message then.

On July 19, 2017, the President again met with Lewandowski alone in the Oval Office. The President raised his previous request and asked if Lewandowski had talked to Sessions. Lewandowski told the President that the message would be delivered soon.

Trump told Lewandowski that if Sessions did not meet with him, he should tell Sessions he was fired.

Immediately following the meeting with the President, Lewandowski saw Dearborn in the anteroom outside the Oval Office and gave him a typewritten version of the message the President had dictated to be delivered to Sessions.

The message definitely raised an eyebrow for Dearborn. He did not want to ask where it came from or think further about doing anything with it. Dearborn also didn't like being asked to serve as a messenger to Sessions. It made him feel uncomfortable.

Dearborn told Lewandowski that he had handled the situation...

but he did not actually follow through with delivering the message to Sessions.

OBSESSION WITH SESSIONS

Within hours of the meeting with Lewandowski, the President gave an unplanned interview to the New York Times.

Sessions should have never recused himself, and if he was going to recuse himself, he should have told me before he took the job, and I would have picked somebody else.

Sessions's recusal was very unfair to the President. How do you take a job and then recuse yourself? If he would have recused himself before the job, I would have said, "Thanks, Jeff, but I can't, you know, I'm not going to take you".

It's extremely unfair, and that's a mild word, to the President.

Days later, the Washington Post reported...

The Washington Post
Sessions Discussed Campaign-related Matters with the Russian Ambassador

That evening, Priebus called Hunt.

Would you want Sessions to be fired or would he resign?

The President would have to fire him...

...but what would he gain by firing Jeff? There was an investigation before and there would be an investigation after.

DEPARTMENT OF JUSTICE

The following morning Trump tweeted...

Donald J. Trump
@realDonaldTrump

A new INTELLIGENCE LEAK from the Amazon Washington Post, this time against A.G. Jeff Sessions. These illegal leaks, like Comey's, must stop!

Donald J. Trump
@realDonaldTrump

So many people are asking why isn't the A.G. or Special Council looking at the many Hillary Clinton or Comey crimes? 33,000 e-mails deleted?

Later that morning, the President ordered Priebus...

You have to get Sessions to resign immediately. The country has lost confidence in Sessions and the negative publicity is not tolerable. I need a letter of resignation on my desk immediately. Sessions has no choice. He must immediately resign.

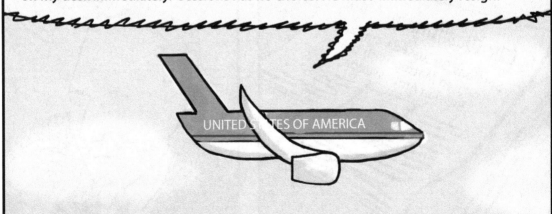

UNITED STATES OF AMERICA

Priebus warned...

If you fire Sessions, you could never get a new Attorney General confirmed. The Department of Justice and Congress would turn their backs on you.

I could make a recess appointment to replace Sessions.

Back at the White House, Priebus called McGahn.

I don't want to pull the trigger on something that is all wrong.

Ignore the President's order.

Later that day, the President followed up with Priebus.

Did you get it? Are you working on it?

Working on it, Sir.

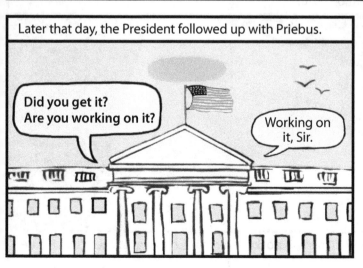

Working on **not** getting it.

It would be a calamity if Sessions resigned because the Attorney General and the Associate Attorney General would also resign.

I'll wait until after the Sunday shows. That'll prevent the shows from focusing on the firing.

By the end of that weekend, the President agreed not to ask Sessions to resign.

Trump tweeted...

Donald J. Trump ✔
@realDonaldTrump

Attorney General Jeff Sessions has taken a VERY weak position on Hillary Clinton crimes (where are E-mails & DNC server) & Intel leakers!

Donald J. Trump ✔
@realDonaldTrump

Why didn't A.G. Sessions replace Acting FBI Director Andrew McCabe, a Comey friend who was in charge of Clinton investigation.

Sessions prepared another resignation letter...

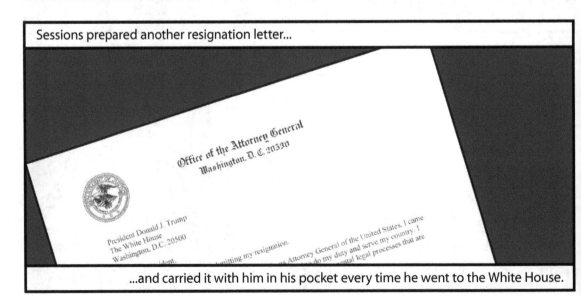

...and carried it with him in his pocket every time he went to the White House.

TRUMP TOWER MEETING EMAILS

By June 2017, the President became aware of emails setting up the June 9, 2016 Trump Tower meeting. The Trump Campaign had previously received a document request from the Senate Select Committee on Intelligence (SSCI) that called for...

"[a] list and a description of all meetings" between any "individual affiliated with the Trump campaign" and "any individual formally or informally affiliated with the Russian government or Russian business interests which took place between June 16, 2015, and 12 pm on January 20, 2017."

The President directed aides...

Do not disclose the emails.

... and edited a press statement for Trump Jr. describing the meeting.

Let's go with the adoption of Russian children.

Communications advisors Hope Hicks and Josh Raffel met with Ivanka and Jared.

The emails are **very** damaging. Inevitably they will leak.

The best strategy is to be proactive. Release the emails to the press.

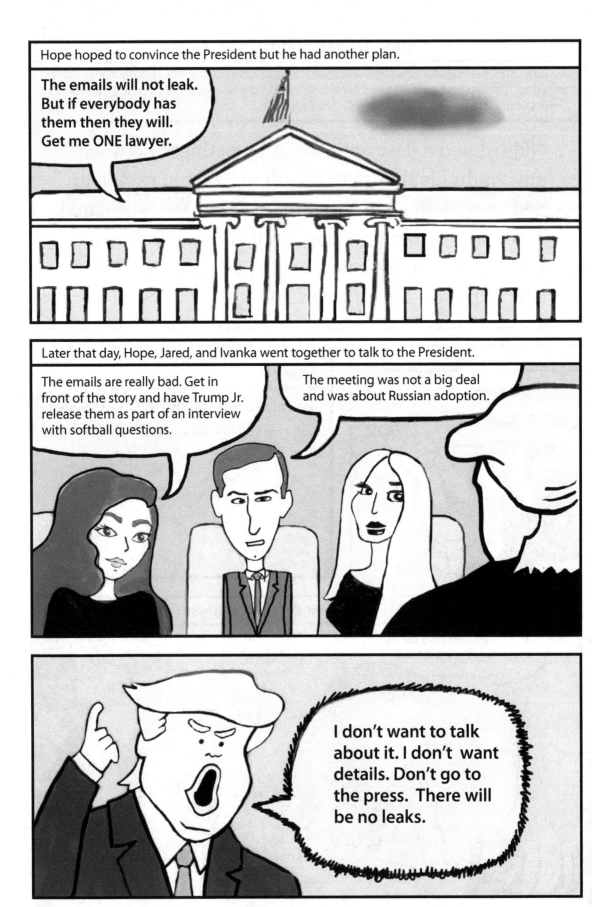

While overseas, Hope learned that the New York Times was working on a story about the June 9 meeting. She told the President and he directed her not to comment. Later in the day he summoned Hope.

What was the meeting about?

I was told the meeting was about adoption.

Just say that.

On the flight home Hope obtained a draft statement to be released by Trump Jr. Hope brought it to the President.

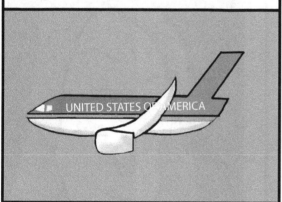

I was asked to have a meeting by an acquaintance I knew from the 2013 Miss Universe pageant with an individual who I was told might have information helpful to the campaign.

This says too much. Say only that he took a brief meeting and it was about Russian adoption.

Hicks texted Trump Jr. a revised statement.

It was a short meeting. I asked Jared and Paul to stop by. We discussed a program about the adoption of Russian children that was active and popular with American families years ago and was since ended by the Russian government, but it was not a campaign issue at that time and there was no follow up.

Trump Jr. texted back.

I want to add the word "primarily" before discussed.

Before the President's flight landed, The New York Times published its story about the meeting with Trump Jr.'s statement.

Trump Team Met With Lawyer Linked to Kremlin During Campaign

Natalia Veselnitskaya

It was a short meeting. I asked Jared and Paul to stop by. We primarily discussed a program about the adoption of Russian children that was active and popular with American families years ago and was since ended by the Russian government, but it was not a campaign issue at that time and there was no follow up.

Soon Trump Jr. posted redacted images of the emails setting up the June 9 meeting on Twitter. The New York Times reported that he did so after being told that The Times was about to publish the content of the emails.

The media reported that the President had been personally involved in preparing Trump Jr.'s initial statement to the New York Times. White House Press Secretary Sarah Sanders provided the answer.

The President certainly didn't dictate the statement.

He weighed in, offered suggestions like any father would do.

The President met with reporters for the New York Times.

I didn't know anything about the meeting at the time. As I've said — most other people, you know, when they call up and say, 'By the way, we have information on your opponent,' I think most politicians — I was just with a lot of people, they said, 'Who wouldn't have taken a meeting like that?'

THE FINAL SESSIONS

From summer 2017 through 2018, the President attempted to have Attorney General Sessions reverse his recusal, take control of the Special Counsel's investigation, and order an investigation of Hillary Clinton. He tweeted...

 Donald J. Trump ✔
@realDonaldTrump

There is ANGER & UNITY over a lack of investigation of Clinton and the Comey fix. DO SOMETHING.

 Donald J. Trump ✔
@realDonaldTrump

The Russian Witch Hunt Hoax continues, all because Jeff Sessions didn't tell me he was going to recuse himself. I would have quickly picked someone else. So much time and money wasted, so many lives ruined... and Sessions knew better than most that there was No Collusion!

 Donald J. Trump ✔
@realDonaldTrump

I put in an Attorney General that never took control of the Justice Department, Jeff Sessions.

That day, Sessions issued a press statement.

 Office of the Attorney General
Washington, D. C. 20530

I took control of the Department of Justice the day I was sworn in .... While I am Attorney General, the actions of the Department of Justice will not be improperly influenced by political considerations.

Sincerely,

Jefferson B. Sessions III
Attorney General

The next day, the President tweeted a response...

 Donald J. Trump ✔
@realDonaldTrump

'Department of Justice will not be improperly influenced by political considerations.' Jeff, this is GREAT, what everyone wants, so look into all of the corruption on the other side including deleted Emails, Comey lies & leaks, Mueller conflicts. Come on Jeff, you can do it, the country is waiting!

November 7, 2018, the day after the midterm elections, Sessions resigned at the President's request.

The New York Times

January 25, 2018

Trump Ordered Mueller Fired, but Backed Off When White House Counsel Threatened to Quit

The next day, the President's personal counsel called Don McGahn's attorney.

The President wants McGahn to put out a statement denying he had been asked to fire the Special Counsel.

PERSONAL COUNSEL

PRIVATE

McGahn's attorney discussed the matter with McGahn. Then he called the President's personal counsel.

McGahn will not make a statement.

Priebus went on television.

I have never heard the President say he wanted the Special Counsel fired.

MEET THE PRESS

The President approved.

You did a great job on Meet the Press.

The Press wanted to know...

Did you ask McGahn to fire Mueller?

Fake news, folks. Fake news. A typical New York Times fake story.

The Washington Post

January 26, 2018

Trump moved to fire Mueller in June, bringing White House counsel to the brink of leaving

McGahn planned to resign but never informed the President.

The President ranted to his trusty White House Staff Secretary, Roger Robert Porter.

The article is bullshit! McGahn leaked to the media to make himself look good. He's a lying bastard.

Tell McGahn to create a record to make clear that the President never directed him to fire the Special Counsel.

If he doesn't write a letter, then maybe I'll have to get rid of him.

Porter delivered the message to McGahn. McGahn responded...

The media reports are true. The President was insistent on firing the Special Counsel.

You may get fired if you don't write the letter.

I will not write the letter.

John F. Kelly, chief of staff, scheduled time for McGahn to meet with him and the President. The morning of the meeting, the President's personal counsel called McGahn's attorney.

PERSONAL COUNSEL

PRIVATE

The President is going to be speaking with McGahn. Whatever happens at the meeting, McGahn cannot resign.

Soon the President began the meeting.

The New York Times story does not look good. You need to correct it.

I never said to fire Mueller. I never said fire.

This story doesn't look good. You need to correct this. You're the White House counsel.

I never told you I was going to resign but otherwise the Times story is accurate.

Did I say the word 'fire'?

What you said is, 'Call Rod. Tell Rod that Mueller has conflicts and can't be the Special Counsel.'

I never said that.

I merely wanted you to raise the conflicts issue with Rosenstein and leave it to him to decide what to do.

I did not understand the conversation that way and instead I heard, "Call Rod. There are conflicts. Mueller has to go."

Would you do a correction?

No.

What about these notes? I've had a lot of great lawyers, like Roy Cohn. I never had a lawyer who took notes.

I keep notes because I'm a real lawyer. Notes create a record and are not a bad thing.

Later that day, the President's personal counsel called McGahn's attorney.

The President is fine with McGahn.

VERY WARM FEELINGS

The President privately asked advisors to pass messages to Flynn.

November 2017, Flynn began to cooperate with the Special Counsel's Office. He withdrew from a joint defense agreement he had with the President. Flynn's counsel told the President's personal counsel and counsel for the White House...

Michael Flynn can no longer have confidential communications with the White House or the President.

Later that night, the President's personal counsel left a voicemail to Flynn's counsel.

I understand your situation, but let me see if I can't state it in starker terms.... It wouldn't surprise me if you've gone on to make a deal with ... the government. ... If ... there's information that implicates the President, then we've got a national security issue, ... so, you know, ... we need some kind of heads up. Um, just for the sake of protecting all our interests if we can. ...The President has very warm feelings toward Flynn.

Flynn's counsel returned the call and reiterated that Flynn could no longer have communications with the White House or the President. The personal counsel responded.

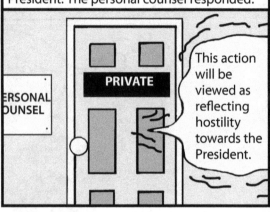

This action will be viewed as reflecting hostility towards the President.

On December 1, 2017, Flynn pleaded...

Guilty

...to making false statements pursuant to a cooperation agreement.

Will you pardon Flynn?

We'll see what happens. I don't want to talk about pardons. Let's see.

I can say this... When you look at what's gone on with the FBI and with the Justice Department, people are very, very angry.

MY MAN MANAFORT

On June 15, 2018, Manafort appeared before a scheduled court hearing on whether bail should be revoked based on new charges that he tampered with witnesses while out on bail. The press wanted to know...

Will you pardon Manafort?

It was never discussed, but I wouldn't take it off the table. Why would I take it off the table?

Hours later, Manafort's bail was revoked. The President tweeted...

Donald J. Trump ✓
@realDonaldTrump

Wow, what a tough sentence for Paul Manafort, who has represented Ronald Reagan, Bob Dole and many other top political people and campaigns. Didn't know Manafort was the head of the Mob. What about Comey and Crooked Hillary and all the others? Very unfair!

The President's personal lawyer, Rudolph Giuliani, gave interviews.

When the whole thing is over, things might get cleaned up with some presidential pardons.

In another interview...

Although the President should not pardon anyone while the Special Counsel's investigation is ongoing, when the investigation is concluded, he's kind of on his own, right?

When it's over, hey, he's the President. He retains his pardon power. Nobody is taking that away from him.

Don't you think yours and the President's comments could signal to defendants that they should not cooperate in a criminal prosecution because a pardon might follow?

Certainly not intended that way.

The President tweeted...

Donald J. Trump ✔
@realDonaldTrump

Bob Mueller is totally conflicted, and his 17 Angry Democrats that are doing his dirty work are a disgrace to USA!

Donald J. Trump ✔
@realDonaldTrump

Paul Manafort worked for Ronald Reagan, Bob Dole and many other highly prominent and respected political leaders. He worked for me for a very short time. Why didn't government tell me that he was under investigation. These old charges have nothing to do with Collusion — a Hoax!

Manafort is a brave man for refusing to break.

Flipping almost ought to be outlawed.

THE PARTY LINE

During the Trump Campaign, the media began questioning Trump's connections to Russia. Michael Cohen, Trump's loyal lawyer, followed the "party line".

Mr. Trump has no business in Russia.

Michael knew.

Protect the Boss and the Boss will take care of you.

In December, 2015 plans were discussed for Trump to travel to Russia to advance the deal.

I'm gonna need your passport, Boss.

TRUMP

During the summer of 2016, Cohen continued to pursue the TrumpMoscow Tower project.

Keep me up to date, Michael.

Sure thing, Boss.

How's the Ivanka Spa going?

Good, Boss.

TRUMP

Cohen reached out to Peskov's* assistant requesting assistance in moving the project forward.

How can we assist?

*Peskov: Putin's deputy chief of staff and press secretary.

In early May 2017, Cohen received requests from Congress...

...to provide testimony and documents in connection with congressional investigations of Russian interference in the 2016 election.

While working on the documents, the President's personal counsel had extensive discussions with Michael.

Do not contradict the President.

Keep the statements short and tight.

The Boss loves you.

Michael submitted the documents to Congress with several false statements. He didn't worry because everyone who knew he was lying was part of the Party Line.

I briefed Mr. Trump on the Trump Moscow Tower project three times.

I did not consider asking Mr. Trump to travel to Russia.

I did not receive a response to an outreach to the Russian government.

The project ended in January 2016, before the first Republican caucus or primary.

In the months leading up to his congressional testimony, Cohen continued to meet with the President's personal counsel.

You're protected as long as you don't go rogue.

The investigations will be over by summer or fall of 2017.

When questioned by a New York Times reporter Michael stayed on script.

Mr. Trump has no business in Russia. The TrumpMoscow Tower Project ended in January 2016.

Cohen knew what to do when a porn star spoke.

My name is Stormy. Stormy Daniels.

Michael Cohen arranged a $130,000 payment during the campaign to prevent a woman from publicly discussing the alleged sexual encounter she had with Donald Trump.

BREAKING NEWS

Cohen knew to protect his boss at any cost. Michael released to the Press...

In a private transaction in 2016, I used my own personal funds to facilitate a payment of $130,000 to [the woman]. Neither the Trump Organization nor the Trump campaign was a party to the transaction with [the woman], and neither reimbursed me for the payment, either directly or indirectly.

The President responded...

I don't know her. Fake news. I knew nothing about any payments. She's not my type.

The President's personal counsel passed on a message to Michael...

PRIVATE

My client thanks you for what you do.

On April 9, 2018, FBI agents working with the U.S. Attorney's Office for the Southern District of New York executed search warrants on Cohen's home, hotel room, and office.

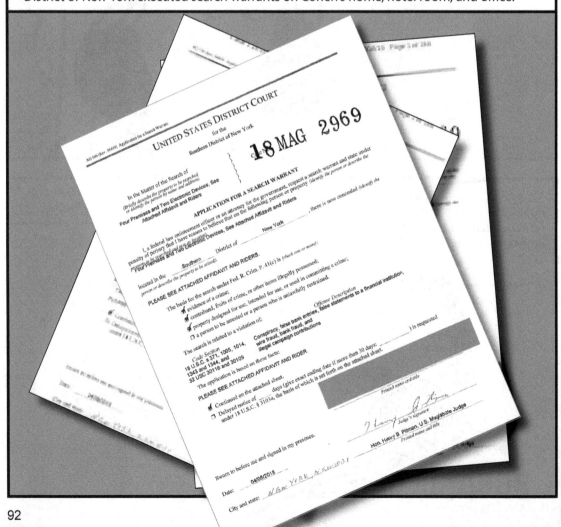

The President was interrupted at a meeting. The President responded...

Just heard that they broke into the office of one of my personal attorneys — a good man.

These searches are a real disgrace. It's an attack on our country, in a true sense. It's an attack on what we all stand for.

Meanwhile, the FBI seized everything out of Michael's home, hotel room and office.

I'm an open book.

The FBI will discover Boss knew about the payments to women. I have a recording of him saying so!

And all those false statements to Congress will be discovered!

The President checked in.

How's it going? Hang in there. Stay strong.

Michael met with the President's personal attorney.

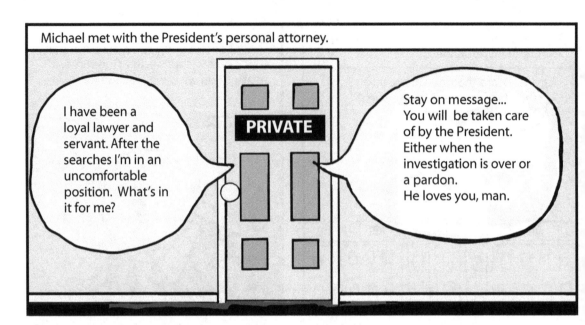

I have been a loyal lawyer and servant. After the searches I'm in an uncomfortable position. What's in it for me?

PRIVATE

Stay on message... You will be taken care of by the President. Either when the investigation is over or a pardon. He loves you, man.

Michael repeated the Party Line.

Protect the Boss and the Boss will take care of you...

The Boss was pleased and tweeted...

Donald J. Trump ✔
@realDonaldTrump

Michael is a fine person with a wonderful family. Michael is a businessman for his own account/ lawyer who I have always liked & respected.

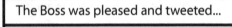

Donald J. Trump ✔
@realDonaldTrump

Most people will flip if the Government lets them out of trouble, even if it means lying or making up stories. Sorry, I don't see Michael doing that despite the horrible Witch Hunt and the dishonest media!

Will you pardon Michael Cohen?

Stupid question.

It's far too early to be thinking about that.

July 20, 2018

The New York Times

Michael Cohen Secretly Taped Trump Discussing Payment to Playboy Model

The President tweeted...

Donald J. Trump ✓
@realDonaldTrump

Inconceivable that the government would break into a lawyer's office (early in the morning) — almost unheard of. Even more inconceivable that a lawyer would tape a client — totally unheard of and perhaps illegal. The good news is that your favorite President did nothing wrong!

August 21, 2018, Michael Cohen pleaded...

Guilty

in the Southern District of New York to eight felony charges, including two counts of campaign-finance violations based on the payments he had made during the final weeks of the campaign to women who said they had affairs with the President.

During the plea hearing, Cohen stated...

I worked at the direction of the candidate in making those payments.

The Boss was not pleased. He tweeted...

Donald J. Trump ✓
@realDonaldTrump

I feel very badly for Paul Manafort and his wonderful family. Unlike Michael Cohen, he refused to 'break'—make up stories in order to get a 'deal.' Such respect for a brave man!

On September 17, 2018, the Special Counsel's Office submitted written questions about the Trump Tower Moscow Project to the President. Attached was Cohen's written statement to Congress and the Letter of Intent signed by the President. The Office wanted to know...

The timing and substance of discussions he had with Cohen about the project

Whether they discussed a potential trip to Russia

Whether the President at any time directed or suggested that discussions about the Trump Moscow project should cease

Whether the President was informed at any time that the project had been abandoned

The President submitted a written response.

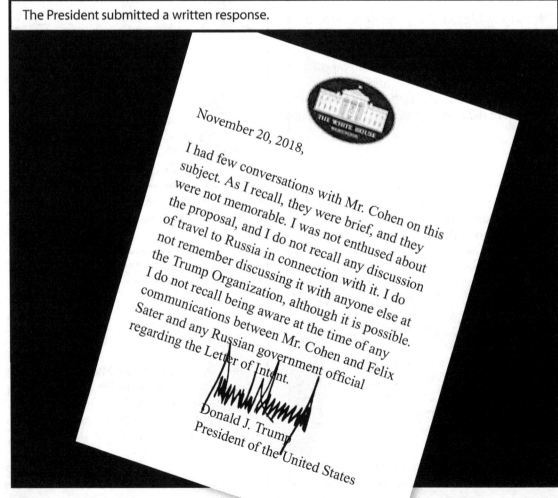

November 20, 2018,

I had few conversations with Mr. Cohen on this subject. As I recall, they were brief, and they were not memorable. I was not enthused about the proposal, and I do not recall any discussion of travel to Russia in connection with it. I do not remember discussing it with anyone else at the Trump Organization, although it is possible. I do not recall being aware at the time of any communications between Mr. Cohen and Felix Sater and any Russian government official regarding the Letter of Intent.

Donald J. Trump
President of the United States

Because the President did not answer the questions, the Office submitted them again. The President's personal counsel responded...

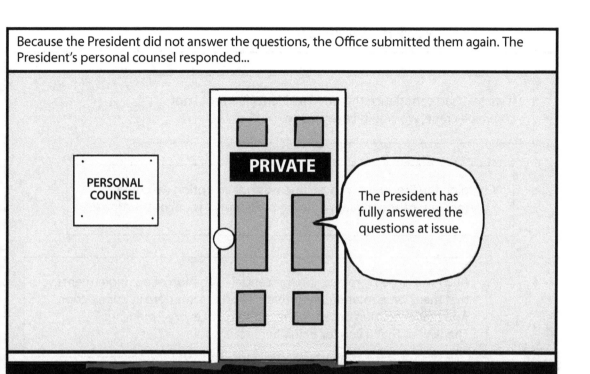

PERSONAL COUNSEL

PRIVATE

The President has fully answered the questions at issue.

Donald J. Trump ✓
@realDonaldTrump

'Michael Cohen asks judge for no Prison Time.' You mean he can do all of the TERRIBLE, unrelated to Trump, things having to do with fraud, big loans, Taxis, etc., and not serve a long prison term? He makes up stories to get a GREAT & ALREADY reduced deal for himself, and get his wife and father-in-law (who has the money?) off Scott Free. He lied for this outcome and should, in my opinion, serve a full and complete sentence.

Michael Cohen is a rat.

If we had had confidence that the President clearly did not commit a crime, we would have said so.

Charging the President with a crime was not an option we could consider. You cannot charge a sitting president. It is unconstitutional.

And I will close by reiterating the central allegation of our indictments, that there were multiple, systematic efforts to interfere in our election. And that allegation deserves the attention of every American. Thank you. Thank you for being here today.

Obstruction of justice is punishable
whether or not
an underlying crime has been committed.

11 OBSTRUCTIONS OF JUSTICE

1. Trump Campaign denies Russia connections. As late as June 2016 the Trump organization was planning a TrumpMoscow Tower.

2. Trump asks Comey for loyalty and to go easy on Flynn.

3. Trump pressures Sessions.

4. Trump terminates Comey.

5. Trump suppresses information on a meeting with a Russian agent at Trump Tower.

6. Trump further pressures Sessions to take control.

7. Trump freaks about Mueller's appointment and tries to revoke it.

Call Rod, Tell him Mueller has to go. Call me back when you do it.

8. Trump dictates to Lewandowski ...

...there were no Russians involved. I know that for a fact because I was there, He didn't do anything wrong except he ran the greatest campaign in American history.

...and tells him to deliver the message to Sessions.

9. Trump orders McGahn to put out a statement denying he had been asked to fire the Special Counsel.

This story doesn't look good. You need to correct this. You're the White House counsel.

10. Trump praises Manafort and hints at a pardon.

Manafort is a brave man. He doesn't break.

11. Trump tries to intimidate Michael Cohen and his family.

Cohen's a rat.

Agalarov, Aras

Russian real-estate developer; met Donald Trump in connection with the Miss Universe pageant and helped arrange the June 9, 2016 meeting at Trump Tower.

Agalarov, Emin

Performer, executive vice president of Crocus Group, and son of Aras Agalarov; helped arrange the June 9, 2016 meeting at Trump Tower.

Bannon, Stephen (Steve)

White House chief strategist and senior counselor to President Trump (Jan. 2017–Aug. 2017); chief executive of the Trump Campaign.

Christie, Chris

Former Governor of New Jersey. Confidant of the Donald Trump.

Cohen, Michael

Former vice president to the Trump Organization and special counsel to Donald Trump who spearheaded an effort to build a Trump-branded property in Moscow. He admitted to lying to Congress about the project.

Comey, James Jr.

Director of the Federal Bureau of Investigation (Sept. 4, 2013–May 9, 2017).

Deripaska, Oleg

Russian businessman with ties to Vladimir Putin who hired Paul Manafort for consulting work between 2005 and 2009.

Dhillon, Uttam

Attorney in the White House Counsel's Office (Jan. 2017–June 2018).

Flynn, Michael T.

National Security Advisor (Jan. 20, 2017 - Feb. 13, 2017), and Trump Campaign advisor. He pleaded guilty to lying to the FBI about communications with Ambassador Sergey Kislyak in December 2016.

Gates, Richard (Rick) III

Deputy campaign manager for Trump Campaign, and longtime employee of Paul Manafort. He pleaded guilty to conspiring to defraud the United States and violate U.S. laws, as well as making false statements to the FBI.

Goldstone, Robert

Publicist for Emin Agalarov who contacted Donald Trump, Jr. to arrange the June 9, 2016 meeting at Trump Tower between Natalia Veselnitskaya and Trump Campaign officials.

Rudolph William Louis Giuliani, KBE

American politician, attorney, businessman, and public speaker who served as the 107th Mayor of New York City from 1994 to 2001. He acts as an attorney to President Donald Trump.

Hicks, Hope

White House communications director (Aug. 2017–Mar. 2018) and press secretary for the Trump Campaign.

Hunt, Jody

Chief of staff to Attorney General Jeff Sessions (Feb. 2017–Oct. 2017).

Kelly, John

White House chief of staff (July 2017–Jan. 2019).

Kilimnik, Konstantin

Russian-Ukrainian political consultant and long-time employee of Paul Manafort assessed by the FBI to have ties to Russian intelligence.

Kislyak, Sergey

Former Russian ambassador to the United States and current Russian senator from Mordovia.

Kushner, Jared

President Trump's son-in-law and senior advisor to the President.

Lewandowski, Corey

Campaign manager for the Trump Campaign (Jan. 2015–June 2016).

Manafort, Paul Jr.

Trump campaign member (March 2016 – Aug. 2016) and chairman and chief strategist (May 2016–Aug. 2016).

McCabe, Andrew

Acting director of the FBI (May 2017–Aug. 2017); deputy director of the FBI (Feb. 2016–Jan. 2018).

McGahn, Donald (Don)

White House Counsel (Jan. 2017–Oct. 2018).

Miller, Stephen (Steve)

Senior advisor to the President.

Page, Carter

Foreign policy advisor to the Trump Campaign who advocated pro-Russian views and made July 2016 and December 2016 visits to Moscow.

Papadopoulos, George

Foreign policy advisor to the Trump Campaign who received information from Joseph Mifsud that Russians had "dirt" in the form of thousands of Clinton emails. He pleaded guilty to lying to the FBI about his contact with Mifsud.

Podesta, John Jr.

Clinton campaign chairman whose email account was hacked by the GRU. WikiLeaks released his stolen emails during the 2016 campaign.

Porter, Robert

White House staff secretary
(Jan. 2017–Feb. 2018).

Priebus, Reince

White House chief of staff (Jan. 2017–uly 2017); chair of the Republican National Committee (Jan. 2011–Jan. 2017).

Rosenstein, Rod

Deputy Attorney General (Apr. 2017–present); Acting Attorney General for the Russian election interference investigation (May 2017–Nov. 2018).

Sanders, Sarah Huckabee

White House press secretary (July 2017 -).

Sessions, Jefferson III (Jeff)

Attorney General (Feb. 2017–Nov. 2018); U.S. Senator (Jan. 1997–Feb. 2017); head of the Trump Campaign's foreign policy advisory team.

Spicer, Sean

White House press secretary and communications director (Jan. 2017–July 2017).

Trump, Donald Jr.

President Trump's son and executive vice president of the Trump Organization; helped arrange and attended the June 9, 2016 meeting at Trump Tower.

Trump, Ivanka

President Trump's daughter; advisor to the President and former executive vice president of the Trump Organization.

Veselnitskaya, Natalia

Russian attorney who advocated for the repeal of the Magnitsky Act and was the principal speaker at the June 9, 2016 meeting at Trump Tower with Trump Campaign officials.

Yates, Sally

Acting Attorney General (Jan. 20, 2017–Jan. 30, 2017); Deputy Attorney General (Jan. 10, 2015–Jan. 30, 2017).

CPSIA information can be obtained
at www.ICGtesting.com
Printed in the USA
LVHW012344291020
670159LV00007B/146